Slim Goodbody's
GOOD HEALTH GUIDES

STAYING WELL

By Slim Goodbody

Photos by Chris Pinchbeck
Illustrations by Ben McGinnis

Consultant: Marlene Melzer-Lange, M.D.
Pediatric Emergency Medicine
Medical College of Wisconsin
Milwaukee, Wisconsin

GARETH**STEVENS**
GS
PUBLISHING
A Member of the WRC Media Family of Companies

Please visit our web site at: www.garethstevens.com
For a free color catalog describing Gareth Stevens Publishing's
list of high-quality books and multimedia programs, call
1-800-542-2595 (USA) or 1-800-387-3178 (Canada).
Gareth Stevens Publishing's fax: (414) 332-3567.

Library of Congress Cataloging-in-Publication Data

Burstein, John.
    Staying well / by Slim Goodbody.
        p. cm. — (Slim Goodbody's good health guides)
    Includes bibliographical references and index.
    ISBN-13: 978-0-8368-7744-1 (lib. bdg.)
    1. Diseases—Juvenile literature. 2. Children—Diseases—Juvenile literature. I. Title.
R130.5.B873   2007
613—dc22   2006032769

This edition first published in 2007 by
Gareth Stevens Publishing
A Member of the WRC Media Family of Companies
330 West Olive Street, Suite 100
Milwaukee, WI 53212 USA

Photos: Chris Pinchbeck, Pinchbeck Photography
Illustrations: Ben McGinnis, Adventure Advertising

Managing editor: Valerie J. Weber
Art direction and design: Tammy West

Printed in Canada

1 2 3 4 5 6 7 8 9 10 10 09 08 07 06

TABLE OF CONTENTS

Words that appear in the glossary are printed in **boldface** type the first time they occur in the text.

Body Blues

Let us learn about diseases
That cause fevers, coughs, and sneezes,
Runny noses, chills,
    and shakes,
Scratchy throats and
    bad earaches.
All those nasty colds
    and flues
Giving us the body blues.

4

Have you ever had to stay home from school because you were sick? Have you ever had a bad tummy ache or eyes that itched like crazy?

You probably answered yes to more than one of these questions. After all, getting sick is a normal part of growing up.

Luckily, your body has an amazing ability to heal itself. Let's explore how your body gets sick and how it gets well.

Something to Think About

If you break the word disease into its two syllables, you get *dis-ease*. *Dis-ease* means not feeling at ease, in other words, feeling sick.

Enemies!

Most diseases are caused by **germs**. Germs are tiny enemies that attack your body like an invisible army. They slip in through your nose, your mouth, your eyes, or cuts in your skin. This germ attack is called an **infection**.

Once germs get in, they make more and more of themselves. As the germs increase, you get sicker.

Two kinds of germs are viruses and bacteria. They both cause diseases, but these germs are different in several ways:

1 Bacteria are bigger than viruses.

2 Most bacteria are harmless. Many actually help your body. For example, bacteria in your **small intestine** help you **digest** your food.

3 Most viruses are harmful.

4 Medicines called **antibiotics** can kill the bacteria.

5 Antibiotics do not work against viruses. Few medicines kill viruses. Your body must do all the work of getting rid of viruses itself.

Something to Think About

To see bacteria, you must use a **microscope** that makes them look one thousand times bigger than they really are. To see viruses, you need a special microscope that makes them look one million times bigger than they really are!

Body Battle

Even though there are millions of harmful germs around you, most of the time you stay healthy. Your body has many ways to defend itself and fight back against germs.

Your skin is your first line of defense. It keeps most germs out. Sometimes germs slip in through cuts or other openings, such as your eyes, nose, or mouth, however.

When germs get past your skin, a group of **defenders** rushes to the rescue. These are your **white blood cells**. They search for the germs and destroy them.

Your nose may also help out. It starts running with a gooey fluid called mucus. Mucus is sticky. It traps germs. Once the germs are stuck in the mucus, you can blow your nose and get rid of them. Germs in your throat also get stuck in mucus. When you cough up mucus, out go the germs.

You may get swollen **lymph nodes** on the sides of your neck. Swollen nodes usually mean that there is an infection in or near your head. Your nodes have trapped some of the germs. Your body also makes special chemicals called antibodies that help kill or control the germs.

As your body battle rages, your temperature may rise above normal, which is 98.6 degrees Fahrenheit (37 degrees Celsius). When your temperature rises, it is called a fever.

The body battle may go on for hours, days, and even weeks. Finally, your defenders win, and you get well.

Something to Think About

Not all fevers are helpful. If they are too high (above 102°F or 38.8°C) or last too long, they can be harmful. Your doctor may give you medicine to bring down the fever.

Lots of Shots!

To help your **immune system** fight germs, your doctor can give you an immunization shot. Scientists have created immunizations for the following diseases — chicken pox, polio, diphtheria, strep pneumonia, tetanus, whooping cough, measles, German measles, mumps, hepatitis, and others. There are more immunizations being tested every day.

An immunization contains a germ from a disease. The germ is either dead or too weak to hurt you. Once this germ is inside you, your body can learn how it looks and works. With this information, your immune system creates a special army of defenders. These defenders are ready to fight this germ if it ever gets in again. They have learned its tricks, and they can spot an **invasion** quickly.

Immunizations do not work 100 percent of the time. Some people still get the disease. If that happens, however, their **symptoms** will probably be milder. Some immunizations last for a lifetime. Sometimes you need a booster shot every few years. A booster shot makes the original immunization work longer. Sometimes you must get an immunization every year.

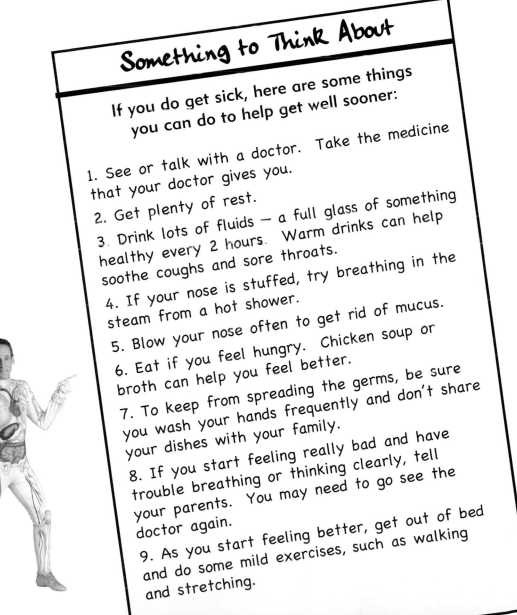

Something to Think About

If you do get sick, here are some things you can do to help get well sooner:

1. See or talk with a doctor. Take the medicine that your doctor gives you.
2. Get plenty of rest.
3. Drink lots of fluids — a full glass of something healthy every 2 hours. Warm drinks can help soothe coughs and sore throats.
4. If your nose is stuffed, try breathing in the steam from a hot shower.
5. Blow your nose often to get rid of mucus.
6. Eat if you feel hungry. Chicken soup or broth can help you feel better.
7. To keep from spreading the germs, be sure you wash your hands frequently and don't share your dishes with your family.
8. If you start feeling really bad and have trouble breathing or thinking clearly, tell your parents. You may need to go see the doctor again.
9. As you start feeling better, get out of bed and do some mild exercises, such as walking and stretching.

Be a Body Buddy

If you take really good care of your body and practice healthy habits, you will not get sick as often.

So be a buddy to your body and . . .

1 Eat healthy foods every day. You need a combination of whole grains, fruits, vegetables, dairy products, meats, and beans.

2 Get 8 to 10 hours of sleep every night.

3 Get plenty of exercise.

4 Keep your hands clean. Dirty hands can carry germs into your mouth, nose, eyes, or cuts in your skin. Washing kills these germs before they can start trouble.

To do a good job, use soap and warm water. Keep washing for about 15 seconds or about as long as it takes to sing the "Happy Birthday" song twice. Wash especially before you eat and after you use the bathroom.

Cold Facts

- Colds are the most common illness.
- Grownups get about two to four colds a year.
- Children get six to ten!

Here is what happens when you get a cold:

1. Germs attack your nose, throat, and ears.
2. You may not feel bad right away. It can take 2 to 3 days to start feeling sick.
3. Your head feels stuffy.
4. You feel tired.
5. Your nose begins to drip.
6. You may run a low fever.
7. You may start sneezing and coughing.
8. Your throat or ears may become sore.
9. Your eyes may water.
10. You may not feel like eating.
11. You will be better in about a week.

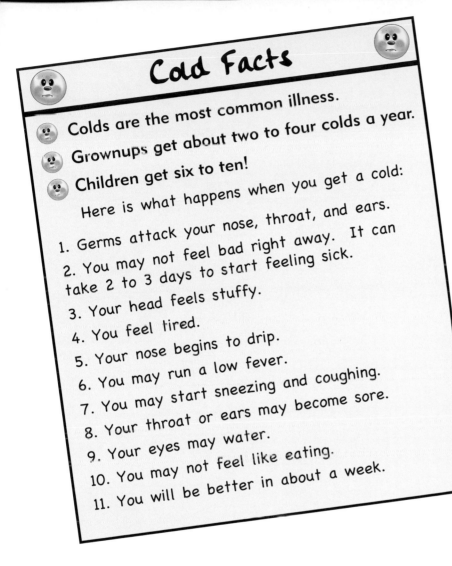

Something to Think About

There are over two hundred different viruses that can cause colds but no immunization to prevent them. No one has figured out a way to fight all two hundred with one shot.

Ear Aches and Eye Itches

Ear infections are the second-most common childhood illness. Some ear infections are caused by viruses and some by bacteria.

Your ear has three parts — the outer ear, the middle ear, and the inner ear. Most ear infections happen in the middle ear. Your middle ear is connected by a tube to the back of your throat and nose. This tube lets air in and out. It can also let in germs. If you have a cold or an **allergy**, this tube may become blocked. You can get an ear infection in one or both of your ears.

outer ear   middle ear   inner ear

tube to throat and nose

Here is what can happen next:

1. Germs get stuck inside the middle ear.
2. Fluid builds up.
3. The germs in the fluid multiply quickly.
4. The infection gets worse.
5. Your ear feels like a balloon ready to pop. It hurts!
6. You may get a fever.
7. You may have trouble hearing, chewing, and sleeping.
8. You will be better in 3 to 6 days.

Eye Sore

Pinkeye is the most common eye problem children get. This disease gets its name from the way it makes your eye look. The white part of your eye and the inside of your eyelid become pink or red. Viruses or bacteria can be to blame.

You can get pinkeye in one eye or both. Your eyes usually do not hurt, but they itch a lot. Try not to rub your eyes. Rubbing will not help and can even make the itch feel worse.

Pinkeye can also cause:

1 Swelling

2 A goopy liquid to form in your eyes

3 A pasty crust on your eyelids when you wake up.

Often a doctor will give you eyedrops or cream to help speed the healing. Medicines called antibiotics will help if bacteria are to blame for the infection. A warm or cool washcloth placed over your closed eyes can also help you feel better. It takes about one week to get better.

Something to Think About

Pinkeye spreads very easily. Imagine your friend has pinkeye and has just touched her eyes. If you touch her hands and then touch your own eyes, you can catch pinkeye!

Crummy Tummy and Tender Throat

The stomach flu is another common childhood illness. When the viruses or bacteria that cause this disease attack your tummy, different things can happen:

1 You might get squeezing pains called stomach cramps.

2 You might feel dizzy and sick to your stomach.

3 You might need to throw up.

4 You might get **diarrhea**.

One of the only good things about the stomach flu is that it does not last too long. Sometimes it is called the "twenty-four-hour flu." However, it may take a day or two more to feel better. If you feel hungry, be sure to eat foods that are gentle on your tummy like toast, crackers, bananas, and rice.

The stomach flu does not cause all stomachaches. There are many other reasons people get bellyaches:

1 Eating too much junk food

2 Eating food that is too spicy or greasy

3 Eating too little food

4 Eating too fast

5 Not eating enough fruits and vegetables

6 Feeling worried about something

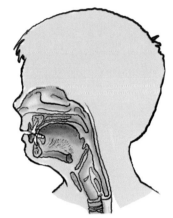

Steps of Strep

Strep throat is a painful illness caused by bacteria. When you have strep throat:

1. It takes about 3 to 5 days to feel sick once the bacteria get in.
2. Your throat will get very red and sore.
3. The back of your throat will have many white or reddish spots.
4. It will be hard to swallow.
5. The sides of your neck may swell.
6. You will probably have a fever.
7. You may have a headache or tummy ache.
8. Your breath may smell bad.
9. You will feel tired.
10. You will be better in about a week and a half.

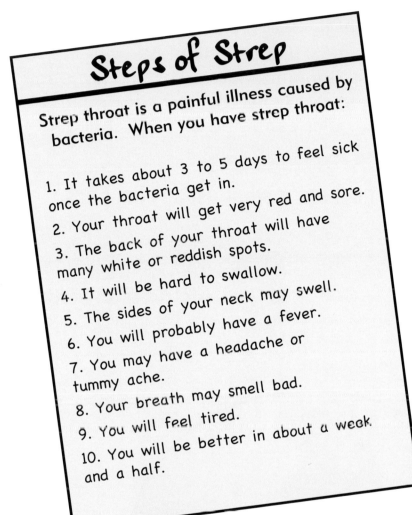

Something to Think About

When you get strep throat, a doctor will give you antibiotic medicine to kill the bacteria. You must take this medicine. If you do not, the germs can spread to other parts of your body and make you even sicker. After taking the medicine for 24 hours, you will not feel so bad.

Flu Season

The flu is a very serious illness. It usually attacks people during the winter months. We call this time of the year the "flu season." Getting a flu immunization each year in the fall helps. The shot that protects you one year will not work the next, however. The viruses that cause the flu keep changing, so scientists are always inventing new immunizations.

If you do get the flu, here is what usually happens:

1. You run a fever.
2. You feel chills.
3. Your body aches.

4. You may get a cough.
5. You might get an earache.
6. You will be better in a week or two.

Nasty Pneumonia

Pneumonia is a nasty infection of one or both lungs. When you have pneumonia, here is what happens:

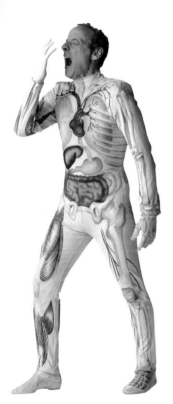

1. Fluid builds up in your lungs.
2. It becomes harder to breathe deeply.
3. You may feel that you cannot catch your breath.
4. You probably will have sharp chest pains.
5. You run a high fever and have chills.
6. You may cough up mucus.
7. You may be sick to your stomach.
8. It may take several weeks to get better.

Something to Think About

You can help stop the spread of a disease by using a tissue. If you are sick and sneeze or cough, you send germs flying from your nose or mouth. If you use a tissue, it will catch the germs before they escape into the air where others can breathe them in.

Spots and Dots

Chicken pox starts off like a cold, with a runny nose, sneezing fits, or cough. Then things get worse.

Here is what usually happens:

1 After 1 or 2 days, a rash begins with rose-colored spots on your chest and face.

2 The rash spreads. Some people get just a few spots. Spots cover other people from head to toe. Some even get spots in their ears and mouth!

3 The spots develop a small, fluid-filled **blister** on top. The blisters are very itchy.

4 Within a week, all the blisters crust over and form scabs.

5 In about one week, the blisters all heal, and you are fine.

While you heal, try not to scratch the blisters. They can tear and leave scars. They can also become infected with other germs. Some people soak in a lukewarm bath with oatmeal in it to help with the itchiness.

Whooping It UP

The real name for whooping cough is pertussis. It got its nick-name because of the whooping sound people make right after they cough. Whooping cough can be so serious that young children sometimes have to go to the hospital for special care.

Whooping cough starts like a regular cold. For about two weeks, you will have a runny nose and a low fever. You will

sneeze and cough a bit. Then things get worse. For about the next two weeks, here is what happens:

1 Your coughing spells become longer and can last for more than a minute.

2 You may not get a chance to catch your breath. Cough medicine will not help.

3 Your may turn red or purple.

4 You may vomit.

5 At the end of the coughing spell, you may gulp air in so quickly it sounds like a whoop.

6 It may take several months to get all better.

Bacteria cause whooping cough. To fight them, you will need to see your doctor to get antibiotic medicine.

Something to Think About

We have immunizations for chicken pox and whooping cough. The chicken pox immunization works so well that 85 percent of the people who are immunized never get chicken pox. Sadly, not everybody gets these immunizations. Because they do not get immunized, people still suffer from these illnesses when they do not need to.

Mumps and Measles Meanies

Viruses cause mumps and measles. Not many people get these diseases anymore because of immunizations. If you do happen to get them, here is what will happen:

Mumps

1 You will feel swelling around your ears and jaw.

2 It will start on one side of your face and may then spread to the other.

3 Your cheeks will puff out. You may look a little like a hamster with food in its cheeks.

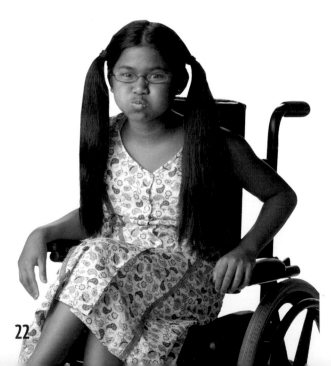

4 The swelling can make chewing, swallowing, and talking very painful.

5 You may run a fever up to 103°F (39.4°C).

6 You may not feel like eating.

7 You will feel weak and tired.

While you are healing, eat soft foods and drink plenty of fluids. Warm or cold packs on your cheeks may help. You do not have to stay in bed, but be sure to take it easy for a while.

Measles

1 You will get a runny nose and a cough.

2 Your eyes will get red and hurt if there is a bright light.

3 You may run a fever as high as 105°F (40.5°C).

4 A reddish-brown rash appears, usually on your forehead.

5 The rash spreads down over your face, neck, and body.

6 After 3 days, the rash reaches your feet.

7 Three days later, the rash begins to fade.

8 You will be better in about a week.

While you are getting better, it helps to rest in a dark room so your eyes do not hurt.

German Measles

German measles is not as serious as measles.

1 You will get a mild fever for 1 or 2 days.

2 You will get swollen lymph nodes.

3 After 2 or 3 days, rose-pink spots will appear, not reddish-brown ones like measle spots.

4 The spots will spread from your face to the rest of your body.

5 As they spread downward, your face will clear.

6 You will be better in about 3 days.

This disease is sometimes called the "three-day measles."

Something to Think About

Before there was an immunization for mumps, about 200,000 people got mumps each year in the United States. Now that we have a mumps immunization, there are fewer than 1,000 cases a year.

Allergy and Asthma Attacks

Allergies are a special kind of problem. They are not caused by germs. They are caused by mistakes made by your own immune system. Instead of helping you, your immune system is actually causing the trouble.

For reasons that nobody fully understands, your body thinks that something harmless is harm**full**! For example, you can be allergic to flowers, dust, peanuts, milk, pets, or antibiotics.

If you come close to something you are allergic to, your immune system sends chemicals into your blood.

Different things can happen then:

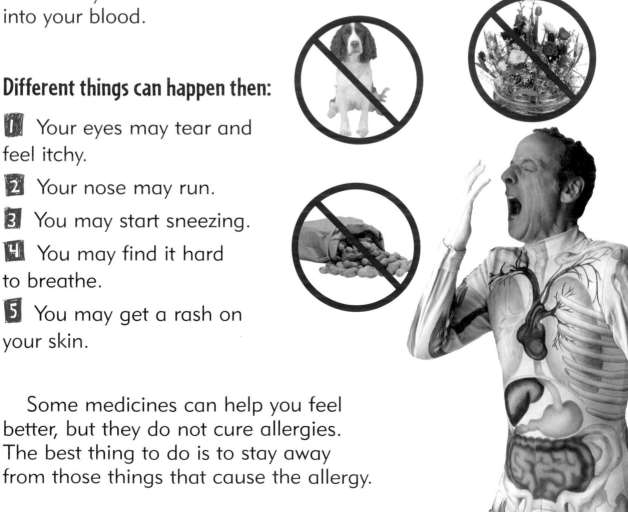

1 Your eyes may tear and feel itchy.

2 Your nose may run.

3 You may start sneezing.

4 You may find it hard to breathe.

5 You may get a rash on your skin.

Some medicines can help you feel better, but they do not cure allergies. The best thing to do is to stay away from those things that cause the allergy.

Asthma

Asthma is a lung disease that causes breathing problems. Many of the things that cause allergies also cause asthma, but these two problems are not the same. Asthma is much more serious.

Asthma is not a disease that people are cured of in a week, a month, or even a year. If they have asthma, it may last their whole life long. Asthma is the most common, long-term health problem children have.

If you have asthma, every so often, you will have an asthma attack, or flair. Sometimes these flairs will be mild. They may only cause some coughing and wheezing. Sometimes the flair will be serious and scary. If the flair is serious, here is what will happen:

1 The muscles lining **airways** in your lungs will tighten up.

2 The airways in your lungs will narrow.

3 The airways will get clogged with mucus.

4 It becomes harder to breathe, and it can hurt to try.

5 You may cough a lot and wheeze.

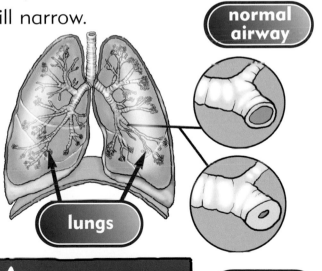

normal airway

lungs

narrow airway

25

Diabetes

When you eat, your body changes some of the food into a special kind of sugar. The name of this sugar is *glucose*. Your body uses the glucose for energy.

If you have diabetes, something goes wrong. Your body is not able to use the glucose, so it builds up in your blood. Too much glucose in your blood can make you very sick.

Nobody knows for sure how someone gets this disease. We do know that you cannot catch diabetes from someone else.

There are two kinds of diabetes — Type 1 and Type 2. Type 1 diabetes is more serious than Type 2. People with Type 1 diabetes must get shots every day to control the disease. They must also be very careful about the foods they eat. Type 1 diabetes cannot be prevented. Doctors do not know who will get it and who will not.

Someone with Type 2 diabetes may or may not need a daily shot. They can sometimes control the disease by eating the right foods and getting enough exercise. Doctors believe many cases of Type 2 diabetes could be prevented if more people stayed at a healthy weight.

Something to Think About

Only grown-ups used to get Type 2 diabetes. Now some children are getting it because more and more kids are overweight. Doctors believe that being very overweight can lead to Type 2 diabetes.

If you have Type I or Type 2 diabetes, you will:

1 Feel tired because your body is not getting the energy it needs.

2 Go to the bathroom a lot because your body is trying to get rid of the extra sugar in your blood by passing it out of your body in your urine.

3 Drink a lot to make up for all that urinating.

If you have Type I or Type 2 diabetes, you will need to:

1 Cut down on fast food

2 Cut down on sugary drinks

3 Choose healthy snacks

4 Get plenty of exercise

5 Have regular check-ups with a doctor.

Kids with diabetes may have to do some special things, but it does not have to stop them from doing what they love. They can still play sports, go out with their friends, go on trips, and have lots of fun.

Singing a Healthy Tune

Now that you have learned about different illnesses, you are better prepared to fight them.

Here is why:

1 Knowing about something makes it less scary. You know what to expect.

2 Knowing about something puts you in charge. You know what to do.

There are billions of harmful germs in this world, but your body is far stronger. With proper care, it usually heals itself quickly.

If you keep
Your body strong,
Most illnesses
Will not last long.
Those body blues
Will fade, and soon
You'll start to sing a
Healthy tune!

Feel proud of your wonderful body,
and do all you can to keep it healthy.

Glossary

airways — the passages to and from the lungs through which air travels

allergy — a strong reaction to something breathed in or touched that quickly causes sneezing, itching, or rashes

antibiotics — medicines that fight certain kinds of germs like bacteria

blister — a raised bump on the skin that is filled with liquid

defenders — groups that come together to fight off invaders

diarrhea — very watery bowel movements; a bowel movement is the waste that your body makes

digest — to break down food into the chemicals that the body needs to work

germs — tiny living things that can cause diseases

immune system — all the parts of the body that join together to fight off diseases

infection — a sickness or disease caused by germs

invasion — enemies entering, spreading, and trying to take over

lymph nodes — small, jelly bean-sized tissue in the neck, under the arms, and through-out the body

microscope — an instrument with one or more special lenses that make small things look large

small intestine — a tube about 20 feet (6 meters) long that is part of the system that breaks down food in the body. The small intestine connects the stomach to the large intestine.

symptoms — warning signs of trouble in the body, such as spots, sneezing, or tiredness. Most illnesses produce different symptoms.

white blood cells — special cells in blood that fight germs

For More Information

BOOKS

Breathe Easy: Young People's Guide to Asthma. Jonathan H. Weiss (Magination Press)

How I Feel: A Book about Diabetes. Michael Olson (Lantern Books)

Measles. Epidemics (series). Maxine Rosaler (Rosen Books)

Microlife That Makes Us Ill. Amazing World of Microlife (series). Steve Parker (Raintree)

Sugar Was My Best Food: Diabetes and Me. Carol Antoinette Peacock, Adair Gregory, and Kyle Carney Gregory (Albert Whitman & Company)

You Can't Take Your Body to a Repair Shop: A Book About What Makes You Sick. Dr. Fred Ehrlich (Blue Apple Books)

WEB SITES

America Museum of Natural History: Infection Detection Protection
www.amnh.org/nationalcenter/infection
Learn about germs, infections, and the flu and how they spread.

Kids Health for Kids
www.kidshealth.org/kid/ill_injure
Check out the links to topics varying from common colds and the flu to chicken pox and pinkeye.

Slim Goodbody
www.slimgoodbody.com
Discover loads of fun and free downloads for kids and parents.

Note to educators and parents: The publisher has carefully reviewed these Web sites to ensure that they are suitable for children. Many Web sites change frequently, however, and Gareth Stevens, Inc., cannot guarantee that a site's future contents will continue to meet our high standards of quality and educational value. Be advised that children should be closely supervised whenever they access the Internet.

Index

About the Author

John Burstein (also known as Slim Goodbody) has been entertaining and educating children for over thirty years. His programs have been broadcast on CBS, PBS, Nickelodeon, USA, and Discovery. Over the years, he has developed programs with the American Association for Health Education, the American Academy of Pediatrics, the National YMCA, the President's Council on Physical Fitness and Sports, the International Reading Association, and the National Council of Teachers of Mathematics. He has won numerous awards including the Parent's Choice Award and the President's Council's Fitness Leader Award. Currently, Mr. Burstein tours the country with his multimedia live show "Bodyology." For more information, please visit slimgoodbody.com.